Your Strategy Guide:

How to Win and Profit from Penny Auction Sites

E.M. Michels

How to Win and Profit from Penny Auction Sites

ISBN: 1453785051

EAN-13: 9781453785058.

Dedication page.
Mike, Jim and Ellen, Thank you for the time and effort to make this the best book it can possibly be.

Foreword

So, you want to learn how to increase your chances at winning penny auction bids? Good for you! This book was designed to help you realize that worthwhile goal. Even if you are just getting started, by the time you are done reading this guide you should be better prepared for your time playing in this exciting, vibrant new frontier. It will challenge you and hopefully land you some extra dough!

Many people love the idea of a new challenge. It is our competitive nature that has propelled humanity through its many heights over the millenniums. These challenges show up in every part of our being, from the workplace to our personal lives. And nowhere does it appear more than in the games I play.

Make no mistake about it. While the penny auction is a serious business, it has the fun, challenge and thrill of a game. And as I all know, in every game there are winners and there are losers. Which category you fit in will not only depend on luck, but on the strategies you employ.

With that thought in mind, you should realize that any bit of information is gold. If it helps to put you on even ground with most of your competition, then it's platinum. And if it helps you have the edge on some of the other inexperienced users, then I hit a mother lode of diamonds. And that is where this handbook comes in.

"How to Win & Profit from Penny Auction Sites" is meant to provide you with a one stop guide to your penny auctions experience. From what they are, to what strategies you can employ, to learning what to buy and why, this guide will answer every question you can think of in regards to penny auctions. And hope-fully we'll touch on some things you haven't even thought of yet.

The book is broken into several parts. First, I am going to explain what a penny auction is and how it works. Next, I provide the strategies you will need to become a bidding expert by providing you with information to help you protect yourself from scammers who prey on the ignorant. I will suggest what to do when you both win and lose, as well as how you can turn your winnings into entrepreneur gold. Lastly, I provide you with an appendix filled with the various penny auction sites you can visit (as the time of publication) and a glossary of the most used penny auction terms.

One thing I want to make clear early is that this is a reference guide. It is a tool. A tool which is meant to provide you with the information I feel you need to have before you make your first bid. This book has been tailored specifically to take a person with no knowledge of penny auctions and guide them through the learning process.

Even if you have already tried various sites and feel you have a good understanding of how penny auctions work, I highly recommend you to start from the beginning of this book with a clear, open mind. To conclude, read everything! I went through great lengths and countless hours to gather and present this tome of knowledge for your benefit. If you own the eBook version of this guide I recommend you print out a hard copy and write in as many notes in the margins as you feel you are necessary. It may seem a bit unfamiliar at first, but I assure you after a while you won't even notice it. I feel that no matter how well I try to explain this to you, nothing beats your ability to put these statements in your own words, thereby creating a clearer prospective.

Table of Contents

Chapter One

What is an Online Auction?

An online auction provides users with the opportunity to compete for the purchase of an item (new or used). Each individual interested in the item will place a bid, which in turn will drive up its price. Once the auctions timer runs out, the last person to bid is declared the winner (though there are cases where no one may win if the bids did not make it up to a pre-determined reserve price).

Let's look at an example of a traditional auction. Bob wants a new laptop. He goes onto a traditional auction site like eBay which is probably the biggest most well known, and after filtering through the sea of used items and sellers with shady reviews, he finds a brand new laptop with all the bells and whistles. It is the ideal laptop for what he needs for school. Bob does some comparison shopping and finds out that the laptop is worth approximately $1,299 retail. With 3 days left in the auction, the item is currently bid up to only $500.

Bob checks on the item over the next 3 days and finds that the price hasn't gone up at all. Finally he sits down to get "serious" about getting the laptop with about half an hour before the auction ends. Over the next half hour he places a series of bids against to ferret out the weak bidders, who are trying to take "pop shots" at winning the laptop. (Think people that don't really need the laptop so much as it is an impulse buy to them or maybe they hope to buy it at such a low price that they could relist it on the auction site and make a profit on it for themselves.

With only a couple of other people competing against him, Bob will continue to bid in earnest and eventually win the laptop in the last few seconds, with shipping his final price will be $1150.00....***Yippee!***

Ok. So then what is a Penny Auction? Well, like the name implies, It is a type of online auction and like a traditional eBay style auction, the winner will be determined by the highest bidder. The items you will bid on are practically always new, but some sites may but rarely auction used items (if that is the case they are usually clearly marked on the auctions webpage). Most penny auctions will start at a price of zero or one cent with each bid raising the cost of the item by one cent. There are some penny auctions that may have a higher starting price but again these will be rare as it is almost always against their interest to do so.

Penny auctions have two major differences from their more popular cousins. First and most importantly, are the way they utilize bids. Unlike a traditional online auction site, Penny auctions require you to pay for the privilege to make bids for an item. The prices can widely vary depending on the number of bids you purchase (we will discuss buying blocks of bids to lowers your per bid cost later in the book) and which site you buy the bids from. On average, you should find the price of bids to range anywhere from $0.60 to $0.90 each.

The second important difference is the way auction time remaining is handled in a penny auction.

Unlike a traditional online auction, when the timer hits zero and the highest bidder wins, the clock never stops and is always decreasing at a constant rate. Auction timers on a penny auction are dynamic, meaning when you put a bid on an item the auction time is extended by a predetermined number of seconds. This allows other bidders who are interested in the item to have a shot at winning at winning the item as well. This means that no one truly knows when exactly a given penny auction will end. It ends only after a predetermined time period and can be anywhere from a 30 seconds to a few minutes, depending on the auction site.

So on the plus side there are no more bid snipers taking away your bid at the final second (though I will discuss a new type of sniper in our strategy section). On the negative side, you can no longer try and wait until the clock is about to expire and throw in a bid yourself with the hopes of sniping it either. So luck plays a bigger role in winning a penny auction than in a traditional online auction, but. There are some strategies you can employ to help reduce the "luck" factor and hopefully make you a more successful bidder.

Let us look at a new example. Bob wants to purchase a new laptop. But this time instead of going through a traditional online auction site like eBay, he pulls up a list of the current popular penny auction sites.

After doing his research (part of which you are doing now by reading this book) he finds a penny auction website which is showcasing a brand new laptop, with all the comparative features of the laptop in the first example, this similar laptop also retails for $1,299. The auction expires in 4 hours, but unlike a regular auction it has an extended time feature of 20 seconds for every one cent bid. Comfortable with his selection of auction sites, Bob buys a pack of 100 bids for an average cost of $0.60 per bid. You could say that now Bob has 100 bullets to fire off at his target, the new laptop. Bob can use some or all of his bids to try and secure his new laptop, of course the less he uses, the cheaper the laptop will cost him in the end.

Since we will tackle strategy later in this book, let's say for sake of this example, that Bob used his bids wisely and won the laptop for $25.37. He used up 80 of his 100 bids in the process. This

brings his total cost for his brand new laptop to $73.37 (80 bids multiplied by $0.60 per bid equals $48, plus $25.37 for the auction price, equals $73.37).[1] Yes, you read it right! Bob paid only about 6% of the retail cost for his brand new laptop.

Good for you Bob!

For Your Review – Remember these points from this chapter

• Almost all auctions on a penny auction site are for brand new items.

• Unlike regular auction sites, there is only one seller,

the auction site. No sifting through sellers ratings!

• Each penny auction bid costs money. Treat them
with the respect they deserve.

• Every bid someone makes will extend the time of the
auction. The amount of time will be listed on the items
auction page.

• The last person to bid when time runs out is the
winner. Be that person!

If you are like me, the next question you want to ask is,

"How the heck are these guys still in business?"

Let's look at the example I just went through a
little more closely. Bob and his competitors piled up
only $25.37 in bids. However, each penny bid placed
had a nominal value attached to it, which in Bob's case
was $0.60 per bid. Let's assume everyone who took a
shot at this auction paid the same price for their bid

E.M. Michels

packs as Bob. Since each penny bid is worth $0.60, the auction site
made $1,522.20 ($25.37 translates to 2,537 individual penny bids, multiplied by $0.60, equals $1,522.20).

So in this case, the auction site made more than the suggested retail price. No, don't be jealous of them. The penny auction sites have a ton of expenses that will cut into that profit, advertising for example, and re-member not all of their auctions will be profitable.

Alright, let us move on to the different types of auctions you will be competing in.

---

[1] All penny auction items will include a nominal shipping cost. The shipping price should be listed at the bottom of your auction.

Chapter Two

Types of Auctions

Now that you have a clear understanding of what a penny auction actually is it's time to find out what type of auctions you have to work with.

Most penny auction sites feature the traditional penny auction we covered in the first chapter. The site will list a variety of brand new items each with a starting bid of $0.01. Every time a bid is made by a user the amount will increase the auction price by $0.01 and extend the auction timer by several seconds, (anywhere from 5 seconds up to a minute depending on the auction site, though 30 seconds seems the be the most common amount of additional time) when the timer expires, the last bidder wins the item.

Now that you have a good understanding of the basics, let's look at a few other types of auctions you may see during your internet travels.

Note

Remember, here I are just trying to present an overview of what you can expect from the most popular penny auction sites. We'll cover each of these types of auction in a little more depth in our strategy section later on. Right now, I just want you to take note of the choices many sites have to offer you.

The Reveal Price Auction

The reveal price auction (or view price auction) follows all of the tenets of your regular auction with one notable exception. The actual price of the item is hidden from you. If you want a peek at the price, then it is going to cost you a fee, usually in the amount of one bid. So what is the big deal you ask? Well each view also drops the price of the item by a predetermined amount. (The auction items webpage will list what that amount is for the item.)

Once the price is revealed, you will have a pre-determined number of seconds (as listed on the item's webpage) to buy the item. If you are not happy with the current price you find, then you can wait and see if it drops more as other users spend their bids to look at the price and in doing so continue to drive down the price of the item albeit usually one cent at a time.

Remember that every person that uses a bid to look at the price also has the choice of buying the item at that price.

Let's bring up an example. Bob wants to purchase a new iPod. His research shows the iPod retails for $150.00 online and eBay has some new ones as low as $130.00, including shipping and handling. Rather than join the huge school of fish trying to push these prices up, Bob scouts around until he finds a penny auction site which has the item he wants. But hold on here, this isn't a normal penny auction site. This one has nothing but reveal price auctions. Not sure of what they are all about, Bob grabs his handy penny auction reference guide and reads up on reveal price auctions. After spending some time to familiarize himself with these auctions and checking to make sure the site is legitimate (always be mindful of new sites), he likes what he reads and decides to give it a shot.

First he needs to register to the penny auction site and buy some bids. After looking over his purchasing options, he settles on buying a 10 bid pack for $7.00. This will provide Bob with up to 10 "reveals" of his target product. Next he looks over the items auction webpage and sees the retail price for the item is $140.00, but the websites starting sales price is $135.00. The site also charges $5.00 for shipping and handling. He also notes that every time the price is revealed and the person chooses not to purchase the item, the price drops by $0.50.

He clicks on the items show price button and finds that the current price of the item is $126.50. That's good, but not as good as the average price of the vanilla auction sites. Bob decides to wait a few minutes and then try again. The next time he hits the show price button he finds a price of $106.50. Now we're talking.

Bob now has a choice to make. He's slightly under the cost he would have probably paid for eBay, but he could get this for even lower. Here we're just assuming he's happy with the price and buys it now. Bob's total cost for this item is $114.50 (Purchase price of $106.50, plus two bids worth $1.50, plus $5.00 shipping, equals $114.50). When the day is done, Bob saved $15.50. Nice work Bob. All that homework really paid off for you.

But the iPod could have just as easily slipped through Bob's grasp if any of the people that spent the 40 bids driving down the price decided to purchase the item at the price that they saw it at. You can see now where the element of suspense and excitement are coming from, and this is just one reason why these sites are so popular recently and growing tremendously. Of course, it is better that you miss out on an item at a price you don't like than it is to buy it at a bad price, but this is about strategy and I will cover that shortly.

For Your Review – Remember these points from this chapter

• You have to pay a bid to see the price of the item.

• The items price will go down each time someone hits the reveal button.

• The winner of the auction is the one who reveals the bid and buys the item at that price. You only have a set amount of time, usually only 10 or 20 seconds, to decide whether to pay that price for the item.

The Reverse Price Auction

Like the name implies, a reverse price auction starts out at, or close to, the retail price of the item. At the start of the auction the price of the item will begin to decrease by a predetermined amount. At any time during the auction you can buy the item at the current listed price. The auction ends when a person finally decides to buy the item. This is similar to the reveal price auction except that everyone knows the price the whole time.

To take part in these auctions you need to pay a predetermined entry fee. Usually, the price of the fee will vary depending on the value of the product and maybe just a number of bids that you have already purchased. The more expensive the product, the higher the fee or number of bids it will be.

For example, while perusing the internet Bob finds out that one of his favorite movie trilogies is now available on blue ray disc. Rather than pay the retail price of $60.00, our shrewd buyer scans his favorite penny auction sites, eventually finding one with a reverse auction starting in a few minutes.

The fee to take part in the auction is $0.60. After doing some research Bob decides that he can let the price fall $13.25 before he needs to make his move. The auction starts and Bob sits for half an hour as the price slowly ticks down to meet his price. Finally, it reaches his price of $47.35 ($60.00 start price, plus the $0.60 fee, minus $13.25, equals $46.75) and Bob puts in his bid, ending the auction right there. Bob smiles, happy with the discount he received on his purchase.

The auction site makes their money on the difference between what they paid for the item and amount of fees they collected from the participants. In this case, if they acquired the movies for $50.00, the site will need about 85 people to pay a fee for the right to bid and buy the item for them to make a profit.

One thing I would like you to remember in regards to these auctions, there is only going to be one bid made for that item and you want it to be you! These auctions are akin to playing that old game of "Chicken". Only here, the guy who flinches first wins the item!

For Your Review – Remember these points from this chapter

- The auction starts at the retail price and drops in increments over time.
- To take part in the auction you must pay a fee.
- The auction ends when a person makes a bid.

<u>The Lowest Unique Bid Auctions</u>

As the name implies, the winner of this type of penny auction is determined by the lowest lone bidder. This means that not only do you have to be the lowest bidder in the auction, but you also have to be the only one to bid that price. Oh and did I mention that you can't see what everyone else is bidding?

That's right; you are placing your bids here blind. The winner of the auction will provide the lowest unique price (which will be revealed after the auction ends). In these types of auctions you are usually allowed to make several different bids. The more you make, the greater the chance you are the lowest unique bidder. Keep in mind sites may put a cap on the number of bids you can make, so be sure to read the websites rules on this auction.

For example, let's say Bob is interested in buying a new cellular iPhone (Got to keep up with the Joneses). He checks out his favorite penny auction sites and zeroes in on a lowest unique bid number that he thinks may win the auction for him. The auction is expiring in 10 minutes.

After some judicious research, Bob picks up a 5 pack of bids at $0.70 per bid and starts punching in amounts. He decides to spend all of his bids in a row, so he selects his bids starting at $0.01, making his way up to $0.05. When the auction ends, Bob finds out that his bid of $0.04 was the winner! Looking at the results chart, Bob sees that 3 bidders made a bid of $0.01, 2 bidders bid $0.02 and 2 bidders bid $0.03, Bob had the only $0.04 cent bid, 5 bids were made at $0.05 and only one bid was made at $0.06.

Of course this is just an example. The lowest unique price could easily be $100.00, it is only with proper research and tracking can you may an educated guess at what a price may close at, and let's not discount the luck factor.

But for this illustration, let's say Bobs won the auction because he was the lowest solitary bidder, well then congratulations Bob. You are on a roll here today!

For Your Review – Remember these points from this chapter

• The winner of the auction is the one who bids the lowest, unique bid.

• Each bid will cost you a pre-determined amount.

• Unless noted in the websites rules, you can make as many bids as you want.

Note

You may also come across some sites offering a highest unique bid auction, where the highest solitary bid wins the item. In these auctions a maximum bid is usually set and you are allowed to bid anywhere under that amount.

The Seat Auction

Seat auctions are timed auctions which require you to purchase a seat before you are allowed to start bidding on an item. Most sites will ask you to purchase credits which can be used to acquire an auction seat. The price per credit is usually similar to the bid prices in other types of penny auctions, $0.50 to $0.80. The price of the seat is determined by the value of the item you are bidding on. These types of auctions are usually found attached to big ticket items, like a car, plane tickets or vacation packages. Each bid will raise the price of the item by a predetermined amount. Usually the higher the item is worth, more each bid increment will cost.

Most of these auctions will be on a timer. When time runs out, the highest bidder is the winner. Much like normal penny auctions, a last second bid before the timer runs out will result in additional time being added to the auction clock. To keep the auctions from running too long, these types of auctions usually only allow a certain amount of overtime, such as 30 minutes, before they close the auction. The amount of overtime should be posted on either the individual auction webpage or in the terms and conditions of the auction site.

Unlike other penny auctions we've mentioned so far, here you only pay for the seat and the final price of the item (if you manage to be the highest bidder when the timer runs out). The entrance fee allows you to make as many bids as you want on that item. In a lot of ways this most resemble a traditional on-line auction with the exception that the timer is dynamic, at least to a point.

To help control their costs, these auction websites will require a specific number of people to sign up for seats before the bidding will begin. In the case of really expensive items, like a car, you may be waiting weeks for the bidding to begin. Once enough bidders have signed up, it is typical for an auction to contact everyone with the auctions starting date and time. So be ready for that e-mail. There usually are no refunds for your seat. These types of auction are also used in conjunction with a marketing campaign for the website. Nothing brings new traffic to your site like a big ticket flashy item.

Bob's wife notices that they have enough saved in their bank account to go on vacation. She doesn't care where they go, as long as it's warm and has a nice beach. While most people would just jump onto whatever travel site they know about, our Bob starts to run through his list of penny auctions.

Sure enough he finds a trip for two to an all inclusive resort with flight vouchers to Jamaica. The total price of the package is worth $5,000. Doing his research, Bob finds similar vacation packages for $5,500. The auction site will start the auction once they get 1000 bidders who are will to sign up for the $5 fee. So far 896 seats are taken (though soon to be 897). The auction is 5 minutes long with 30 minutes of possible overtime. The bidding will start at zero and move up in $2 increments. Bob registers with the site and pays the $50 fee. A days later, he receives an e-mail from the auction site with the date and time for his auction. At the appropriate time, Bob signs on and takes his virtual auction seat. Over the next five minutes, Bob and the other 999 bidders push the price up to $3,600. Since people still want to put in bids, the auction starts to run into overtime. Each bid during overtime, extends the auction by 15 seconds.

After some more time passes, Bob finds himself up against only one other bidder. They exchange bids for a while until finally Bob prevails with a $4,200 bid. Yah Mon!

That leaves Bob with an $800 savings that can be applied towards picking up some his favorite Jamaican exports, like white rum and blue mountain coffee. Yes Bob sure is the luckiest person in the world.

For Your Review – Remember these points from this chapter
• You must pay a fee for a seat in the auction.

• The auction will usually have a set amount of seats available.

• It is typical for the auction site to contact you with a date and time once they have the appropriate amount of bidders for the auction.

• The auction will usually be on a timer, with a set amount of overtime to allow additional bids.

• You have an unlimited number of bids in the auction.

• The price of the item will move up in increments as mentioned on the auctions item webpage.

Chapter Three

What to Look for in a Penny Auction Site

Jump onto your favorite internet search engine and type in "Penny Auction Site". There are dozens of websites catering to your new favorite pastime. They span across the world, from the U.S., Canada and Europe to far off places such as Bali, Malaysia (and New Jersey).

I mentioned earlier there are scammers out there who will stop at nothing to get your money. So you need to protect yourself as best you can. And I go through everything I feel you need to be wary of in our section on auction scams. But there are other things that you should consider about before you lay down your hard earned money on the legitimate penny auction sites. To that end, I would like for you to ask yourself the following questions when considering a penny auction site.

The first question you always want to answer for yourself is ***does this penny auction site have items that you are interested in?*** Remember each site will most likely require you to make a minimum investment in the form of a pack of bids or credits. This is usually somewhere in the neighborhood of $20 to $30 USD. So it can be important for you to find sites which have several items that interest you, and which are going to be available on a somewhat consistent basis.

So maybe a site is not for you if the only interesting item they have is a $60 cappuccino machine whose past auctions have cost around $35. Keep in mind most legitimate auction sites offer a wide array of items, from gift cards to big ticket electronics.

Another good question to find the answer to before you leap is, ***how long has this penny auction site been in business?*** There are many reasons to ask this particular question. Auction sites that have been in business for a long time are less likely to be scamming their customers but the flip side to this coin is that, newer legitimate auction sites may have to start out small and will only have few bidders. This can work to your advantage, if you know what you are doing. Which leads me to the 2nd part of this question. ***What do the reviews have to say about this auction site?*** This shouldn't be too tough to find out as we are in the information age, and people love to review things, especially people that are getting screwed over by a company. Take the time to read the penny auction blogs and get the answers about what past customers of your target penny auction site have to say about the shipping time, the quality of the merchandise and the customer service. The cost of the bids, and the price of the auction items are your homework but the customer service and the quality of the goods, you will need to rely on past customers.

Does the site have the types of auctions you are looking for? Remember there are many types of auctions out there with the promise of more categories coming down the pipeline any day. It will not matter what products a penny auction site has available if you are not comfortable with the types of auctions they employ. We discuss earlier the types of penny auctions and it always amazes me how many new types are introduced. This makes the auction more exciting but also more dangerous. You must make sure you know all the ins and outs of any type of auction that you are seriously thinking about bidding in. Do not let yourself get blind sided by not knowing the auction basics. When does it end, how will it end and how do you win it. (although the how you win it is almost always by being the last and highest bidder.) the point is make sure you know the answers to these questions and well as any other nuance to the exotic auction types *before* your first bid.

Does the site have enough auctions and users?

Some penny auction sites employ a business model known which I will just call "less is more". These sites may offer only a handful of high quality items for auction each day. Other sites have many products available daily, even multiple copies of the same product, at various levels of quality. A 5 gigabyte iPod compared to a 10 gigabyte iPod for example.

More auctions tend to draw more users, which can translate into a larger deviation in the price of an item. This could mean you will have to make more bids and pay a higher auction cost for the item you want. Meanwhile, a smaller auction site with few items may attract fewer users. However, this does not mean the bids may be much lower. Smaller sites tend to draw more serious users, whose honed skills and research are ideal for these hunting grounds of the smaller types of sites. I will get into this in more detail when you read our chapter on bidding strategies.

What is the average cost of bids? Whether you are a budding entrepreneur or a weekend bargain hunter, make sure you know how much each of your bids is going to be worth before you lay down one dime on that site. Typically nowadays you can expect to pay on average between $0.50 and $0.75 per bid in a pack, depending of course on how many bids are in the pack.

The more expensive the bid pack the higher number of bids. Make sure you divide the cost of the pack by the number of bids you receive to figure out your average cost per bid. Also, remember to check a site's free bonus bid offers. Free bonus bid offers as well as discounts available for purchasing larger bid packs. This can dramatically reduce the price of each of your bids.

Note

Make sure you review what requirements you will need to fulfill in order to gain access to any offered bonus bids. Usually a penny auction site will release bonus bids piecemeal, based on the number of bids you make during auctions. This leads us to an important point.

Go through the penny auction site's terms and conditions. I know what you are thinking, almost no one ever reads the terms and conditions on any service they use. I'll admit this much to you right now, I don't usually review them myself. But, this is one of those few times where you really need to go find that link on the website and read it start to finish…Twice! And maybe even take notes to compare with other sites. If you are not use to looking for the link, just check the bottom of the penny auctions main page. Remember, not all penny auction sites are created equal! So it is very important to know all the rules and resources available to you for a given site.

If you are unsure about something in the Terms and Conditions, make sure you fire off an e-mail to their customer support. They are there to answer your questions. As a matter of fact, this can serve as a good way to gauge the quality of their customer service. Remember there are a ton of sites out there, so if you are uneasy with their terms or their customer service, then move on and keep looking for that site (or sites) which ease any and all of your concerns.

Does this penny auction site deliver items to my country? Europe, over the centuries, has brought to us a plethora of wonderful things such as fish & chips, Swiss cheese and now penny auctions. That's right. The humble beginnings of the penny auction central in the "old" country. As such they have a market which is much more mature when compared to the U.S. market. This means there are many more sites in Europe than in the continental U.S. And while there is nothing wrong with checking out and participating with those sites from across the pond, keep in mind that some penny auctions sites do not deliver items worldwide, so it is important to know what countries they ship to. Just as importantly, if they do ship to your country, then you need to know how much they are going to charge you for shipping. A huge site in the UK is of no use to you if they don't deliver to Canada and the U.S., or if

they charge exorbitant shipping and handling fees to send your item there.

As you will soon see in later in the book, infor-mation gathering, and note taking is vital to your success. So the next question you must ask yourself is ***Does the auction site have a lot of information avail-able to me?*** What you are looking for is as much information as possible, especially as it pertains to closed auctions. You want to know for example, what items sold recently?, at what price? and after how many bidders? Not to mention who was the final bidder. Taking this a step further, you would really like to find out all the bidders names, and take the history as far back as you can get it. What you are looking for are trends, and the best trends are only established with a lengthy history, but more on this later.

Probably the most important question of all and unfortunately the toughest one to answer will be *Is the penny auction site legitimate?*

I will go into greater detail about what to look out for in penny auctions, but for now it suffices to say, endeavors as popular as this are going to draw their fair share of shady characters. I can assure you that this has happened in every popular facet of business from the beginning of time.

From eBay scammers to a bunch of guys buying Manhattan for baubles and animal skins, there are always going to be people out there who want what you have for as little as they can get it. A quick check on eBay under penny auction or any one of the bigger name sites will reveal everyone and their aunt online trying to sell a clone of the software used. Read further and some actually build into the software the ability to scam and cheat people.

The world of penny auctions is a dynamic organism, so I am not going to recommend who to trust. It doesn't make sense because by the time you read this book, new sites will have come and some old sites will be gone.

But you can reasonably protect yourself if you follow my chapter regarding scams and shill bidding. It is not fool proof. But few things in life really are. All I ask is that you set reasonable expectations to a penny auction sites claims and then follow your better judgment. And make sure you read my chapter on what to look out for, hell read it twice, because a penny saved is truly a penny earned.

Note

    Remember if a websites deals seem too good to be true, then it probably is. There is no better way to stress this point.

Chapter Four

Know Thy Enemy

He who is prudent and lies in wait for an enemy who is not, will be victorious – Sun Tzu

The world of penny auctions is made up of thousands of people who all want to achieve the same thing you do, win that auction. Auctions are competitions which bring out the best and worse in all of us. Before you're ready to enter the world of online penny auctions let's get to know the basic personality types you will be facing.

The Newbie

Fresh meat…fat, dumb and ready for slaughter…This is the guy that saw a penny auction site commercial 5 minutes ago and is already signed up and firing off bids. You know this person. Hell, you might have even been this person (but you were smart enough to pick up this book and change that).

Here's one way to pick out the newbie's. Open up a standard penny auction which is about an hour from closing. See if it has bids posted already. Write down those names. Now watch that auction when it starts. Make note of those names as the auction progresses. There is a good chance you will see those people are going to make the number of bets equivalent to a starter bid pack and its associated bonus. Write down "NEWBIE" next to their names and draw a little smiley face for finding an easy mark. You deserve it.

For all of you online poker players reading this, these are the fish you want at your $3-$6 table on a Saturday night. The same applies here in the big world of auctions. Let them shoot their loads off early and often. You know that the real bidding comes after these yahoos are long finished and scrambling for a strategy book that will explain to them what went wrong.

Note

Be careful of the newbie in niche product auctions which do not draw many people. This is a happy hunting ground for the newbie shopper and wannabe vanilla auction reseller. The former is willing to fire off a ton of bets just to get their item. The latter can be pointed out as you get closer to the average auction closing price. Against these types, I know to save our bullets for later on or the next day when the same product will probably be available again.

The Famous Auction Sniper

If you ever bought something on a vanilla auction site, then you know about the auction sniper. They are the bringers of doom and wasted hours in front of your favorite auctions. These infamous characters lay in wait at the end of your traditional online auctions. With one click of the mouse button they steal away your item at the last second, and usually at the lowest amount possible.

Understand the auction sniper is not to be confused with the auction function known as auto-sniping. We'll get to them soon enough. No, these are the people that have the patience and willpower to let that clock drive down to almost the very last second before they post their bid. These experts can lie down quite a bit of confusion and frustration, especially when you have a great number of bids invested in an item.

The auction sniper forces you to remember his name. So fine, show him the respect he deserves. Track him and his bids. Even though he is frustrating, he may reveal a pattern to you that can be used against him. Expect to see his name on many of the same or similar items. He follows very tight patterns, usually reselling the items he wins. He focuses in on a handful of items and knows everything about them, including how long the auctions usually last, how much (or at least a range) the item auctions go for, and what they can expect in a return when they resell the item using other channels.

Just remember, a sniper is best flushed out with either another sniper or bombarding him into submission with automatic bids. I get more into these tactics in our bidding section.

Deadeye – The Penny Auction Auto-Sniper

This is the next evolution of the sniper profile. These new monsters of auctioning mayhem come in two varieties. The first type of sniper is given his abilities by the penny auction sites themselves. I know you're asking yourself right about now, "Did I hear that right?" Yes, you did. Some auction sites allow a bidder to place a certain number of last second bids automatically. Keep in mind though, usually the number of sniper bids allowed per auction is limited and can come with preset conditions.

For example, you may have to set aside a minimum number of auto-bids in order to access your sniper rounds or your sniper rounds may only be available after a certain amount of time in the auction has lapsed, or before a pre-determined price is reached. Whatever the case may be, this has quickly become a favored weapon for those who are worried about lag killing their last second bids.

The second type is known as the software assisted sniper. This tech wiz uses a third party software program to put that bid in at the very last second. These deadeyes have existed on the World Wide Web for years dating back to the early wild old west days of eBay. And now he has brought his sharpshooter show to the penny auction crowds.

What their software does is sync up the clocks of the user's computer and the auction site's webpage. All these whiz kids need to do is adjust some settings to match the conditions of the auction and they are off to the races. They can now sit back and let the software fire off their last second bids.

Like any sniper they are frustrating to go up against. You cannot expect to beat them. The best you can do is sit on pins and needles and hope you can outlast them and if possible avoid them altogether.

The Mac-Daddy Spender

Some call them big spenders. Others call them whales
or orcas. Most people have a friend like the Mac-daddy
spender. They fly first class. They smoke the "good"
cigars and they order the bottled water in restaurants.
These big spenders are the people you want to mark
down in your notes as "toxic when bidding". Why you
ask? Because the Mac-daddies of this world have the
cash, are not afraid to use it like a club to a seals head.
They bully you with large chunks of bids, relentlessly
foiling every attempt made by others for long stretches
of time. Some of these guys may even be willing to bid
up to, shudder the thought, the retail cost of the auction
item!

They show no mercy. They have no mercy in
their hearts to give you. To take another example from
our poker playing kin, these guys like a table that plays
fast and loose. Expect these whales of the auction sites
to fire away like they are having a fun time. And that is
because with many of these titans, that is exactly what

the bidding is to them, entertainment (and the satisfac-
tion of beating everyone else on the block). It is as
much about the thrill of stamping out the competition as
it is about winning the item.

The sooner you identify the big spenders, the sooner
you can get out of their way. That is, unless you're in
the mood to hunt for big game!

The Expert or (The Men Who Stare At Goats)

When I talk about the experts, I do not just
mean the guys who read this book (who should by now
be on their way to that desired level of ability). No, I
am talking about the guys who could write this book.
The ones, who are going to read this reference guide,
take notes and fire off e-mails to me pointing out every
bit of minutia I need to add and omit for our next
edition.

These are the Jedi Knights of the auction world.
They know everything about the auctions they involve
themselves with. From the expected final prices of the
products to the bidding history of the other regulars

they face, the expert makes sure each of his moves are properly calculated ahead of time.

They are by no means infallible. Even the expert will make their share of mistakes and they have long ago accepted the tenet that you can't win every auction. They are gracious with their losses, because they can afford to be.

Against other regulars who understand the work involved in being successful in penny auctions, the expert has built a reputation for his skill and strategy. To others he seems like a guy who often gets "lucky" with his bids.

Again to steal another poker analogy, the penny auction experts are the sharks of the on-line poker world. They understand the psychology behind an individual's betting. And the more you are exposed to them, the more they learn about you and your tendencies.

So how do you find them before they find you?
Well, you can start by reviewing closed auctions of the
items you are interested in. If the site allows it, write
down the top names left in each of those auctions.
Look to see who is up there on more than one auction.

More than likely another trend you will notice
about the group mentioned above is their name will be
associated with similar priced auctions. You are not
likely to see their names on a bid that ran far away from
the average ending auction price.

However, you will likely see them listed on the
really low ones. Those once in a while anomalies
where the bidder pays next to nothing compared to the
average ending auction price. More often than not, the
novice labels these few as just lucky. But odds are this
is the handiwork of an expert.

Joe Average

The world of penny auctions is filled with ex-
traordinary opportunities for great deals and Joe Average is the guy who is going to let it all pass him by.

Like you, he saw an advertisement about penny auctions or heard about it from a trusted friend. He went through the newbie stage and either didn't spend all of his points in one shot or he did and just went out and bought more.

Do you see the problem with this statement yet? You should because what Joe Average will do is continually repeat the same mistakes over and over again. He is the quintessential example of those who are doomed to repeat history because they refuse to learn from it.

If you are tracking him over time (and unless he has deep pockets it is doubtful he will last long enough) he may confuse you with his erratic behavior. There is no pattern there. Joe Average will try a little of each strategy and feature he finds, unconscious of its merits and aware of only one consequence. If he is wrong, then he can just put in some more money or follow the next advertised opportunity that catches his eye.

If you take one thing away with you from this book, let it be this: Don't be like Joe. Learn from your successes as well as your mistakes.

Now that you have met the enemy, let's look at how I am going to beat them in our next chapter on bidding tactics.

Chapter Five

TACTICS

In any endeavor that I partake in, success or failure relies on tactics. I don't care what you are talking about here. Whether it is competing on the field of battle or the field of play, the proper execution of the right tactic will all but ensure your victory.

Unfortunately, few games provide you with a clear road to the "right" tactic and so I am forced to concede that no tactic is foolproof. No victory is ever ensured on a fair playing field. To win at this game, one must be ready to learn all of the tactics available to them. With that knowledge they then can learn to adjust their tactics to the situation at hand.

Read the every changing flow of the bidding correctly and you will more likely come away a winner. Read them wrong and you will pay with your hard earned currency.

So let's look at the various tactics that can be applied and what I think you should do in such situations.

Every challenge is like a game. And every game has rules, resources and players. This guide has endeavored so far to teach you the rules and players of the penny auction world. Now I am going to bring those two facets together by showing the tactics you should employ using the resources available to you for that site.

As I have alluded to many times in this text, the object of this game is to win the prize. And the key to winning that prize is to know when your bid has the best chance of being the last one made for that auction.

For that I need to learn how our opponents are expected to react to a given situation. And to do that I need data. As a matter of fact, I need streams and streams of the stuff. The more information I have on our opponents and the products they are interested, the better our chances will be of winning those auctions.

So where do I start? Good question. Like any other game, once I know the rules and the type of players I will face, I next want to learn whatever history on them and the products they buy.

First, go find a penny auction site which you would be comfortable using real money on. Go on, I'll wait for you. Ready? The first thing I want to do is to try and identify who the regular players are and if possible, what are their tendencies?

The easiest way to gather up a list of the players is check out the site auctions for bid packs. Bid packs auctions, are special auctions where you actually bid on more bids? Talk about a win-win for the auction site huh? If you are successful and disciplined you know exactly how much these bid packs go for. While everyone has to start out buying a bid pack to get in the game, the regulars know that their money is better spent gathering up bid packs at a discount.

Since that is the case, then this is the right spot to start our education. Now that I have our item picked out, I next want to gather up as much information as available. Open the last closed auction for the bid pack you are tracking. Grab a pen and some paper or open up your favorite spreadsheet program. First, we'll add the name of our auction item. For arguments sake, we'll say it is a bidding pack of 100 bids. These bids, if you were to purchase them directly from the site, would be worth $0.70 per bid (or $70 total).

Next, I list any special details about this particular auction. Was it only open to people who never won an auction before? Was there a ban on automatic bids here? Any information I can gather about the auction should be added to a separate notes column or if you are really detailed oriented (thought some might say anal) like me, then you are going to create columns for each of these types of occurrences and mark off yes whenever you come across one of these situations.

Now let's create some column headers. Our first two columns will be the date and time the auction closed, followed by the name of the winner and the price they paid for it. Most sites will also tell you how many bids the winner made, so put that in the next column. Most sites nowadays provide a list of the last 10 to 15 bids made before the auction closed. This information can be a gold mine for picking out our regulars. If this is the case, first make a column called Type of Win. Here you will add how they won their bid (whether it is by a regular, automatic, dreaded sniper attack, etc...).

The next step is easier if you are using a spreadsheet program, but you can work out on paper with only a little more fuss. I are going to assume that if you were savvy enough to buy this book, then you probably know your way around a spreadsheet program. On a separate sheet of paper or spreadsheet, list the name, bid price and type of bid each of the final bidders made along with the date and time the bid closed. If they offer everyone that took part in the auction, then copy down everyone's information. In a separate column note the winner of the auction with something like an x.

Now do that for as many of the 100 bid pack auctions you can find. This could take a significant amount of time. Bid packs are usually very popular on penny auction sites, and why not? You are getting a chance at a great deal on reloading your account at deep discount.

Try to go back at least for 1 month's worth of auctions. Again, I understand this is going to take a while, but every bit of time you spend here, increases the chances that you are going to make winning bids. While you are doing this I want you to take note of any repeat winners you come across.

Now that I have a full spreadsheets worth of information, let's start to do some analysis. The order you do your analysis in does not matter as much as understanding the results, so you can do these next few steps in whatever order you want to.

Let's start by getting a look at what the "average" final price was for each of these auctions. I am going to get a few different views of this price using some simple statistical formulas. Don't worry I'm not a mathematician, and I don't expect you to be either. Just follow the instructions and take long breaks if your eyes start to roll up behind your head.

When I say average price, I mean what is the middle range in final prices for our target item. This information helps us to create an expected value for the auctioned item. Let's start with the simplest of calculations, finding the arithmetic mean. It is as easy as eating PI.

First, get a count of the number of auctions you have. Next, add up the total prices of those auctions. Finally, I divide the number of auctions into the total prices to get the average price.

For example, I wrote down the information for one month worth of auctions for a 100 bid pack from a popular penny auction website. When all was said and done, I had 390 auction results. I added up the final prices of all 390 auctions and came up with a total of $3,795.35. Now I divide the 390 auctions into the total,

$3,795.35 and I get an average final auction price of
$9.73 calculated as (390/3,395.35 = 9.73).

So now I know that the average price of one
month's worth of 100 bid pack auctions was $9.73.
This is a good start, but it is only the beginning of the
road for us. This average includes the lucky (or very
smart) few who won with a really low bid and the few
who for some strange reason just would not stop
bidding and drove the price way out of the ballpark of
reality. Or at least past the fair value of the bids had
they been purchased at the regular price. What I really
would like to see is a range of prices without the two
aforementioned extremes, and from there get an average price in which I can work from.

To do that, I am going to find the mode (or
modes) in our data set of auction prices. The mode is
simply the most frequent number, or numbers, to occur
in a given dataset. For example, if I had a dataset of
1,1,2,3,3,4,4,4,5, then the mode here would be 4 since it
shows up more times than any other number. If the
dataset had two modes, then it is called a bimodal set.

If there were more than two modes, then it is known as multimodal. Are you still with me? If not, go take a break and come back in a little while to reread this section. Otherwise, let's press on.

List the number of times each final price comes up. If you are using a spreadsheet program, then the first thing I want to do is copy the price column and pass that information on a new spreadsheet. Next you want to sort your price column in ascending order (meaning low price to high price). Now that you have all your prices in order, place the number 1 next to each price on your spreadsheet. This should leave you with two columns made up of the final prices and a bunch of ones. For example, if I had a string of numbers 1,2,3,4,5,6,6,6,7,8,9, 10 it would look like this on my spreadsheet.

$1 - 1

$2 - 1

$3 - 1

$4 - 1

$5 - 1

$6 - 1

$6 - 1

$6 - 1

$7 - 1

$8 - 1

$9 - 1

$10 - 1

Now scroll down the list of prices until you come up to a price which repeats itself. Now next to the first price in that group, erase the 1 in the column and put the number equal to the total times that price repeated it. Then you can delete any other rows with that same price.

Using the example above, I stop at the number 6 and count 2 repeat prices for a total of 3 occurrences. So I change the 1 next to first $6 to a 3 and delete the other two rows of $6. Now our spreadsheet should look like the following example.

$1 - 1

$2 - 1

$3 - 1

$4 - 1

$5 - 1

$6 - 3

$7 - 1

$8 - 1

$9 - 1

$10 - 1

Once I have done that for our entire price sheet, I am ready to start trimming the spreadsheet down. In the example I are using it is simple to see that the most common price I find is $6. So $6 is our mode.

Unfortunately, your spreadsheet will not be that easy to trim down. There is a chance you will have multiple modes on your spreadsheet. That is fine. I am expecting this to happen. In our example of 390 prices, I found up to 2 spots where the same price showed up 3 times, and 8 spots where the same price showed up twice.

What I want you to do here is look at your numbers for the desired pattern. In this case I am looking for a block of prices which repeat themselves. That block of numbers is what I are ultimately looking for. Don't worry, you will find those numbers if you wrote down at least 100 prices.

Let's take our above example and add a little more to it.

Say it looked like this:

$1 - 1

$2 - 1

$3 - 0

$4 - 1

$5 - 1

$6 - 3

$7 - 2

$8 - 5

$9 - 4

$10 - 2

$11 - 3

$12 - 1

$13 - 1

$14 - 1

$15 - 0

$16 - 1

$17 - 1

$18 - 0

$19 - 1

$20 - 0

Looking at the example above it is easy for us to see that the block I am looking for is between the $6 nd $11. And that is our bidding target. With this basic chart I can now start to dig deeper into the numbers.

Remember that list of name's I told you to write down? Well now I am ready to put that work to use. Go back and find the names of the winners from $6 to $11.

Chapter Six

Value of Research

When doing your research, try to keep the following questions in mind. Everyone should fall under one of these categories. Do they know when to stop bidding?

Newbie and Joe Average – Probably not. If you know how many bids come in your sites bid packs, you can probably count down to the newbie's last bid.

Snipers – The auction sniper is purposely waiting for the last second to make that bid. They are difficult to track without having some history on them. Be assured the sniper knows when to pack up and look for easier targets.

Auto-Snipers – Unlike regular snipers, auto snipers can provide us a little more information. It all depends on the rules of the auction site. Keep in mind their sniper rounds could be tied into a block of auto bidding. Also, some expert snipers will use this feature to fake people out of the bidding. They will usually start with a string of regular bids and then switch to sniper rounds toward the end of their bidding run. The sniper wants you to believe that the bidding has reached a price point where their sniper rounds will bridge them to their auto-bids. This hopefully discourages any bidders who were not planning to go much further into the bidding.

Mac Daddy Spender – They usually don't know when to stop bidding. Of course, this is because they don't care so much about the discount. They just want to win. Expect these guys to come out firing fast and often.

The Expert – While the Mac Daddy Spender was spending the opening rounds stepping on the hopes and dreams of every newbie they could find, the expert went to get a nice hot cup of coffee. When they get back, the Sniper may wait to see if everyone is going to run out of steam or just move on to the next auction.

What are they bidding on?

Newbie and Joe Average – They fall into two categories for the most part. The first group goes after the big ticket items, like TV's and game consoles. Here's one way to find a bunch of them. If the previous auction closed lower than average, on the next similar auction you probably pick out a bunch of newbie's and Joe's all hovering around that lower price waiting to bid. The second group will go after the items which no one else seems interested in. They are just happy to win something.

Everyone Else – You will find them mostly in popular and/or big ticket auctions. Most of these guys are resellers who are trying to gather up some inventory on the cheap. You could occasionally find a Mac Daddy Spender looking to rule over the bidding of a $50 gas card, but those occasions should be few and far in between.

When are they online?

Newbie and Joe Average – Much like online poker, the weekends bring in a stream of people looking for something to do other than mow their lawns. Expect to see a list of novices and Joe's parading around your favorite auction sites during peak weekend and holiday hours.

Mac Daddy Spender – The "MDS" wants a crowd as well as the win. They have obnoxious names which are 15 characters long and were made to be seen. Expect them to be around during peak times when they aren't playing the poker tables.

Everyone Else – The remaining three groups are around at all times, day or night. You might be able to glimpse a few experts during the peak times, but these are probably the dangerous few who armed with a ton of information on their targets and cash reserves to wither out mistakes.

Will they use bully bidding tactics (Are they going to take my lunch money today?)

Newbie – Most newbie's can't be bullies simply because they just don't bring enough bids to bully anyone around. However, they are the ones who typically get bullied around the most by more experienced bidders.

Joe Average – This group may be one of the toughest to gauge. If Joe Average spent 10 minutes reading the strategy section that most auction sites provide, then he may have loaded up for bear. If it is a popular item, you can probably pick out the novice Joe's trying to bully early, or if they have a little more knowledge, you can find them auto-bidding heavy right after a nice round number. Just check out how many auto bidders start their string of bids at price points such as the $1.00 mark. Joe Average can be tough to bully if they have purchased a big enough bid pack.

Fortunately, I know Joe usually only uses one strategy at a given time, so if, you have some recent info on his bidding style you will know how to handle him.

The Snipers (Both Types) – The snipers are too subtle to bully their opponents. Their job is to wear their prey down. Auto snipers don't like bullies because they can eat a bunch of their shots earlier in the bidding then they may want. This is most evident when a sniper starts peppering in regular bids between his sniper shots. It probably means the sniper is worried they will run out of sniper bids before their auto bid gets to kick in.

Mac Daddy Spender – The MDS are the prototypical bully. They can and probably will be in your face from the moment the auction starts. Mac Daddy's will gleefully push everyone and everything aside, including reason, to get to the prize at the end of the auction. And so they should.

They come armed with a huge supply of bids sitting in reserve for just this event. If you followed this guide and made a list of people who won bid packs, beware of any who are on the Mac Daddy list in your auctions. They love to win cheap bid packs and then throw them at high profile auctions. The Mac Daddy also knows how to defend himself in a fight. They know there are a bunch of auto-bids out there. Some would back down against a long string of auto-bids going dollar after dollar. But the Mac Daddy believes the best defense is an overpowering offense. Those auto bidders are doing nothing except blocking their way to victory. And the only way they know to take them down is by bidding their way past them.

The Expert – Where the Mac Daddy Spender is the hammer, The Expert is the scalpel. Loaded with streams of data and research, The Expert looks to make quick, subtle attacks in places they feel other bidders are overlooking. They are the ones who leave people scratching their heads when a mysterious sniper bid wins the auction.

The Expert makes you believe you were bullied out of an auction only to find at the end they made only a few bids to win. But don't think The Experts can't bring the pain. Most likely they have just as large of a bid reserve as the Mac Daddy Spender. They are just more prudent with its use. And how does The Expert battle a bully? They don't even bother. The Expert knows when to walk away, saving their bullets for the next auction.

Do I bid early and often?

Newbie – The newbie is everywhere. He's new and wants to get in on the "action". Newbie's love to see their names sitting out there on auctions with 4 hours left till the end. They want to feel like they are in the game with everyone else. It's no problem if they don't know all the rules or read any of the strategies.

Joe Average – These guys will lay off the beginning in most cases, unless they read a strategy tip which told them to try and take advantage of the bidding early and if they believed that one, then there they are, wasting bids most of the time.

Snipers – The Sniper waits until the last second to bid. Depending on their level of experience and desire for the item, they may make the mistake of coming into the bidding early. How often they bid will depend on factors such as the number and quality of the competitors they are facing.

Auto-Sniper – They hate to "waste" their bids in the early part of an auction. By design, the auto sniper makes bids only when no one else is prepared to make one. This means they will only burn through their shots as quick as the competition allows. Some savvy bidders may try early to test for auto snipers. However, this could result in losing the auction to an early bidder.

Mac Daddy Spender – Sure! Bet early and often. This is a favored bullying technique of the Mac Daddy. They force everyone to sit there and stare at a string of the same name betting over and over and over again.

The Expert knows a sucker bid when they see one. They have put in their time, done their research and know that very few people actually win in the early bidding. The Expert has the discipline to wait till they have the advantage. And what does The Expert do after he watches someone take home that 60 inch LCD TV for $0.14? They just smile, shake their heads and get ready for their next auction.

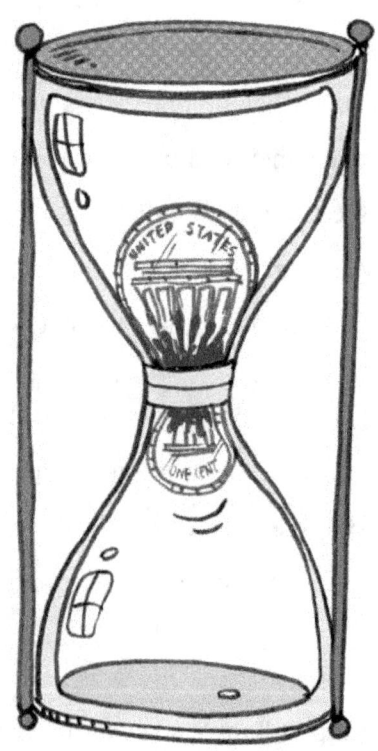

Chapter Seven

Tips to Remember

Here are some helpful tips I have found during our travels which I would like you to remember. Most of these thoughts are just plain common sense. But in any competition, common sense is one of the first things some people throughout the window.

If you are in the market for a new laptop or other high-end device, then penny auctions can be your answer to getting what you want at a discount price. But be REALISTIC! These items are widely popular and draw all kinds of competition. And this book can only help you if are willing to do the research. Even then I recommend you stake yourself to a reasonable budget. Is it possible for you to buy that 42 inch TV with only 22 bids? Sure, it is possible, but your chances really aren't that good if previous auctions have drawn from between 4,000 to 6,000 bids every time.

If you are looking to buy items from penny auctions and resell them, then good for you. I think the reseller road is paved in gold. But remember, Rome was not built in a day and neither will your retail empire. It is imperative that you do all the research I recommended and more. If possible, don't do it alone. Call in favors, bribe/black mail family/friends, do whatever you can to

get as many people gathering as much information for you as possible. There are people out there right now making money while you are reading this. Most of the legitimate successful ones have done their homework and learned well from their experiences.

Eliminate all distractions while you are bidding. Put the dog out, the kids to sleep and the scotch glass down. Get comfortable and turn the phone ringer and the TV off. This is your money I am talking about here. Don't chance losing it is because you were distracted during a crucial bidding phase.

Once you get a feel for your niche on an auction site, start looking to spread your wings to other penny auction sites for the same items. Yes, this means gathering more info and looking for the patterns of a different group of players. But using multiple platforms provides you with more opportunities for those desired items. Of course you also have an edge over much of your competition because of the research you did earlier. You already know who and what to look for in a site, in a product and on your competing bidders. You just need time to learn all about the sites players and then buy some bids.

Be aware of any special deals or auctions your favorite sites may be offering in the future. Any incentive that lowers your cost per bid is important. Also consider partaking in any special auctions that offer rebates on your bids or are free to users who achieve a certain status. These can turn out to be nice little bonuses for you.

Accept the fact that you are going to win some and lose a bunch of auctions. Your object is not to win every auction. The point here is to make a profit. Treat this project like it is a business venture. I'm not saying you should write up a business plan (Well, that's what I would do, but I won't cast stones).

What I am saying here is you need to be realistic with your expectations, business takes time and effort to develop. During that growing period, there is a good chance you are going to eat through a chunk of your budget. If you followed a sound plan, then you will most likely weather out those early storms. If you don't please remember this; never use money you can't afford to lose! Nothing in this world is guaranteed, this venture included. The reward here is not worth risking your rent!

Make sure you keep all of your information lists up to date. The information analyses you gain from those names provide a big edge against many of your competitors. Just remember you are probably not the only one with this information. There are many people out in the world who are just as smart and just as resourceful as you are.

Create a name that stands out from the rest. People should remember you and over time come to dread seeing your name in an auction. And you should never even try to hide your intentions. Be assured that even if you tried, those regulars who are doing their homework will find you. It is only a matter of time before you are measured and weighed, so embrace the notoriety a name like

Mr. IwinBecauseIamsmarterthanyou

Just make sure to leave your ego in the name and not let it out during the auction. Learn from your losses as well as your wins. At some point, examine every auction you take part in. See if you can determine why you lost and what you could have done to prevent it.

The fact of the matter is if you place bidding limitations on yourself, then you are going to take some tough losses. No one wants to be the guy who comes in second. But if you bid on items long enough, it is going to happen. Deal with it and move on. After a few months or so, take a look back at that first month of auctions you took part in. You will probably be surprised at how far you have come in such a short time.

And that brings us to a point I touched on once before. But let us reiterate the point again. Your object is not to win every auction. Don't get me wrong, it would be nice to win them all. It just is not a realistic goal for you. And when you lose, you risk the chance of getting angry, frustrated, sad, as well as host of other emotions that are of no help to you. When this happens it's time to turn the computer off and walk away from the auctions for a while.

To steal yet another poker analogy, don't play on tilt. Always try to keep calm. You will lose money at some point in the most frustrating of ways. Try to keep from losing your cool and throwing good money after bad.

Know the limitations put on you by the site, such as winning bid limits. Some legitimate auction sites will only let you win a certain number of times a week or a month. Make sure to plan for this and any other restrictions.

If the site you use has chat and/or forum functions, ignore them. Many bidders like to use these features to "mess" with their competitions minds. Remember this adage; believe half of what you see and none of what you read in the forums. If you must read the forums, don't post any replies. I feel you should not give anyone a speck of information that can be used against you. Let them ramble about how stupid you were betting against them during that last auction. Let the idiots talk about your mom, your hygiene and your grades in high school.

I am reminded of the old saying, "It is better to say nothing and be thought of as an idiot, then to say something and confirm it." Let the hyenas laugh and

scare away the small birds. You stalk bigger prey
anyway.

Try not to even sign up for the "beginner" auctions that some sites offer. Most of these auctions are
wrought with newbie's who are firing away free bids
they received for signing up. They employ no bidding
strategies and can form what seems like an endless line
of bids.

As we discussed in previous chapters, to be successful in a penny auction you will need a good deal of
discipline. Discipline, not only to put in the time
needed to do your research, but to follow through on
your plan of action. The most important part of this
being to stick with the budget you have decided on
before entering your targeted auction. This is easier
said than done.

As many people will go into a financial venture
with a budget, be it a poker game, trading stocks or
even simply shopping, only to blow past it and later
find themselves trying to rationalize their decision.

How successful you will be in your venture into penny auctions will be directly tied to your ability to stay within the financial limits you set for yourself to win a certain item.

To help you do this, we thought it important to define the two main forces at work which cause people to disregard their spending limits in search of winning that auction.

1. PRIDE - Pride has no gender bias, affecting both men and women equally. Auctions are extremely competitive and when it is one person that you see outbidding you again and again, it is hard not to take it personally. In cases like these, pride will push you to take an attitude of, Screw you buddy, I'm winning this here DVD player.

2. SUNK COST - This is the economic idea that people are influenced by the money in which they have already invested into a given venture and which are unrecoverable as the basis of whether to continue putting more money in. The rationale here is, I am due

to win the auction item because I have already put enough money in to trying to get it. The best place to see Sunk Cost in action is at any slot machine parlor. Here you see many people falling into the Sunk Cost trap. They rationalize that the jackpot is due or coming soon because they have already invested X dollars in the machine. Even though they maybe spending more than planned, this type of person will no want to leave the slot machine now, for fear someone else will win their jackpot. The flaw in this logic is every bet you put into the slot machine carries individual odds of winning the jackpot.

Every time the handle is pulled the odds reset for the next coin. THERE IS NO CUMULATIVE effect at work here. If the odds of winning the jackpot are say 1 in 500, then every wager will be 1 in 500. Wager 10 bets, the odds are not increased to 10 in 500, they are instead (10) 1 in 500 wagers.

In other words, flip a coin 9 times and say you get heads 9 times in a row. What are the chances you

are going to get heads or tails that next flip? The
answer is exactly 50/50.

Recognizing and staying aware of these two
forces should help you avoid falling for them. Remember, though they are alluring, they will guarantee to take
you off track. A pyrrhic victory and a profitable auction
are mutually exclusive.

Do not let your education on penny auctions end
here. Go online and read up as much as you can on the
subject. There are a ton of blogs out there with various
degrees of new and valuable information. But remember to be mindful of these sites. Some of these bloggers
are just marketing companies who work for auction
owners and are just trying to tout a specific auction site.
Be wary of any information site that provides little info,
but lots of publicity for one or a couple of auction
houses.

Chapter Eight

YELLOW FLAG = CAUTION

With the tremendous rise in popularity of this exciting and potentially profitable new auction system, the penny auction is attracting thousands of new customers each day across the world.

Unfortunately, this success has also attracted con artists that set up phony auction sites which are designed to cheat people of their hard earned money. Typically, these crooked sites do not last long. While scam sites are soon discovered as not playing fairly and quickly close down, there are always new ones popping up in their place.

Now I don't want you to fret too much over this. With careful planning and investigation you can possibly minimize and avoid these shady sites all together.

Who cheats and why?

On the surface, who is cheating and why seem like questions with obvious answers. The person who is cheating is the one with direct financial interest in the outcome of the auction, (usually

the seller of the item) and they are doing it because they want to steal your money. But who really is the cheater in a penny auction and why do they want to cheat are much more difficult questions to answer. But they are exactly the answers you need if you hope to avoid these pitfalls.

In the case of a normal on-line auction, like eBay for example, you may see one of these scenarios. An unscrupulous person will put an item up for bid and purposely provide misleading descriptions (i.e. stating it is new when it is actually a used item). Some will even go so far as to "sell" an item and accept payment without ever intending to ship the product to the auction winner. In this case the auction site itself has many rules, policies and systems to identify scam sellers and weed them out. Of course they need to because they are concerned with the integrity and reputation of the site. People continue to use eBay because they know that although there may be the occasional thief out there, for the most part the auctions are reliable. And they are comfortable with the fact that if they come across a scam artist, eBay will make every attempt to fix the problem.

But what if the entire site IS the seller, as is the case in penny auctions. Now the stop gap of the entity making the rules and procedures is gone. There is no law west of eBay, except for the rules each auction site makes for them. This is why it is so important to identify and separate the scam sites from the legitimate ones, thereby minimizing your risks of falling victim to a scammer.

Now as to why an auction site might want to scam their customers, will usually fall into two separate groups. First, is the auction site which is cheating every one of its bidders and is just in it to make a quick buck and close down one step of Johnny Law (These are easy to avoid). The second, and far more dangerous and harder to detect group, are the auction web site operators who only occasionally cheat their customers and only in one almost indiscernible way.

Group 1 – Plain old con artist, without any pre-conceived notions of legitimacy. They have no intentions of delivering any of the items in which they are making available for bidding. They rig the bidding to extract as much money from you as possible. They will be tough to contact and provide false or vague answers to any penetrating questions... This group is from the same ilk as the "work from home," pyramid schemes and the Nigerian money scammers.

Group 2 – These fellows on the other hand may be running a very legitimate looking site. They have auctions which people can win real items on and receive delivery in a reasonable timeframe. These auction sites have a section on their webpage where they can be easily reached (look for a "Contact Us" link at the bottom). Usually they will accept correspondence via email and sometimes even live phone support is available. This group only cheats in one specific way and they see this as not so much as cheating and stealing (which it is), but more of a sound business decision. These sites employ a tactic which is known as "Shill Bidding".

In short, shill bidding is the practice of posting fake bids either by employing an automated method known as a "bot" or clicking on live links. The sites may have various aliases set up to disguise these "shill" bids and so can go virtually undetected by the other real bidders.

Auction sites employ this technique to get a winning item to reach a minimum number of bids before allowing a "real person" to win. This method of scamming can help ensure the auction site will make a profit on each of their bided items The reason why some auction site owners in Group 2 may do this is because they may simply not have enough real people bidding for an item on their auction site.

For example, pretend you are auctioning off a $1,000.00 item, say a big screen TV. At the close of the auction you find that only 50 people bid on your TV and ultimately the item sells for $10.00 (estimating a $0.75 per bid average). That would yield $760.00 (bids plus final purchase cost). These are businesses that are in this venture to make a profit. You wouldn't be in business long if you took a 25% loss on every item you sold. But, if you could extend the time the item was up on auction say by throwing in a few hundred bids, then every bid you add should result in an equal number of real money bids. In this case just 300 more bids would be needed to turn this item from a loss to a break even.

In some cases if the number of real bids is not there to make a profit, shady auction sites may even have the shill bidder win the item, then repost it in another auction later. With the cost of the item already reduced as a result of the real bidders from the previously failed auction, the site now can probably afford to let this auction go unmolested.

How do you protect yourself from scams and cheats?

Cheating can be hard to detect, but there are steps you can take to better protect yourself.

RESEARCH, RESEARCH, RESEARCH

Before placing bid 1 on any auction site, do some fact finding checks on the web and the Better Business Bureau. See if the BBB have logged any complaints about the site. Also check out blogs which mention the auction site. If people feel they have been ripped off by a site, then they are usually more than happy to blog about it and complain. Just keep in mind to try and evaluate people with bad strategy, who lost some money and are just whining from people that appear to have witnessed a real bidding anomaly.

Dip your toe in before committing any real money Most sites offer bonus bids just for signing up and registering. Make sure you use these bids to watch the auctions. Do not commit any money to buying bids until you are confident the auction site is as "safe" as you can reasonably discern. Remember, the auction site makes their money when you BUY the bids, not when you actually use them and most sites do not offer refunds.

Watch the bidders and take notes I recommend watching several auctions on higher priced items, paying close attention to the flow of the bidding. The idea is to look for patterns. If you see a name appear on many auctions, then write it down. Keep track of these names. Do they bid a lot on several different auctions to which they often lose? This is a red flag. Do they win auctions, but clearly overpay? This is definitely a red flag.

In short, the same popularity that makes penny auction exciting also makes them a target for cheaters. You may not be able to 100% protect yourself from them, but if you follow simple rules, you can minimize your risks. If you really want to go overboard in checking out a website, there are advanced techniques that you can employ (that are strictly for the tech savvy) which can monitor a website's traffic and help identify any shill bidding. But at best this is all just a guess, as you will never truly be able to reduce your risks of running across a scam site. Remember no risk, no reward. Just be smart, listen to your gut and you'll be ok.

APPENDIX

Provided here is a list of known penny auction sites, as of this book's publication date. I believe all of the sites below to be legitimate. However, please note I do not vouch for any of the sites on this list. Most of the sites below have not been tested by the author. Besides, I felt it wouldn't be fair to advertise just the sites we like and use often. The purpose of this book was to be educational, not promotional. Just remember to review all the information available about a site (including any site information regarding scams) before committing any money.

Auctions 4 a Cause

https://www.auctions4acause.com

Bargains And Fun

http://www.bargainsandfun.com

Beezid

http://www.beezid.com/

Bid 66

http://bid66.com/

Bidazzled

http://bidazzled.com/

Bid Blink

http://www.bidblink.com

Bid Cactus

http://www.bidcactus.com

Bid Dees

http://biddees.com/

Bid Here

http://www.bidhere.com

Bidoction

http://www.bidoction.com

Bid Pigs

http://www.bidpigs.com

Bid Rivals

http://www.bidrivals.com

Bid Rodeo

http://www.bidrodeo.com/

Bids4Cheap

http://www.bids4cheap.com/

Bid-Save

http://www.bid-save.com/

Bids Tick

http://bidstick.com/

Bid Tent

http://www.poshbid.com/

Bid Trotter

http://bidtrotter.com/

Bid Yell

http://www.bidyell.com/

Big Deal

http://bigdeal.com/

BOOM Bidz

http://www.boombidz.com/

Deal Dash

http://www.dealdash.com/

Dibzees

http://www.dibzees.com/

Dime Divas

http://www.dime-divas.com/

For 10 Cents

http://www.for10cents.com/

Haggle

http://www.haggle.com/

Jeeler

http://jeeler.com/

Lincoln Bidz

http://www.lincolnbidz.com/

Penny Auction Site

http://www.pennyauctionsite.com/

Penny Cave

http://www.pennycave.com/

Penny Lord

http://www.pennylord.com/

Penny Purses

http://pennypurses.com/

Pickle Bid

http://www.picklebid.com/

Pognu

http://www.pognu.com/

Posh Bid

http://www.poshbid.com/

Qui Bids

http://www.quibids.com/

Rocky Bid

http://www.rockybid.com/

Sellmoo

https://www.sellmoo.com/

Skore It!

https://www.skoreit.com/

Smart Bid

https://thesmartbid.com/

Snaglo

http://www.snaglo.com/

Swipe Bids

http://www.swipebids.com/

Swoopo

http://www.swoopo.com/

Unreal Bidz

http://www.unrealbidz.com/

Wavee

https://www.wavee.com/

NOTES:

<u>NOTES:</u>

www.ingramcontent.com/pod-product-compliance
Lightning Source LLC
Chambersburg PA
CBHW072035190526
45165CB00017B/944